100 Angels

A Collection of Handpainted Angels

Presented by

The National Museum of Decorative Painting

100 Angels

A Collection of Handpainted Angels
Presented by
The National Museum of Decorative Painting

Publisher: Jerry Cohen
Chief Executive Officer: Darren Cohen
Product Development Director: Brett Cohen
Art Direction: Andy Jones
Photography: Wes Demarest

Editorial Advisors: Peggy Harris and Linda Heller

Published by:
All American Crafts, Inc.
7 Waterloo Road
Stanhope, NJ 07874

www.allamericancrafts.com

Printed in China
©2011 National Musem of Decorative Painting, Inc.
ISBN 978-0-9819762-9-7
Library of Congress Control Number 2011924850

The National Museum of Decorative Painting was established in 1982 for the purpose of collecting, preserving, and displaying fine examples of decorative painting.

Visit the Museum to experience a dazzling array of both historic and contemporary decorative painting from around the world, including the incredible angels featured in this book.

On behalf of the Museum's Board of Trustees, I would like to thank all the artists who so generously shared their time and talent to create this collection. Without their support, this exhibition and publication would not have been possible.

Enjoy the angels,

Andy B. Jones, Director
National Museum of Decorative Painting

There are nine orders of angels, to wit, angels, archangels, virtues, powers, principalities, dominations, thrones, cherubim and seraphim.

- St. Gregory the Great,
Homilies 540-604 AD

Saint Gregory the Great believed that each person is destined to join one of the ranks of the nine choirs of angels, not as angels, but as God's children by cooperation with his grace and perseverance.

The origin of angels in history is quite complicated, with angels or similar spirit beings found within many cultures throughout the world. Sumerian culture flourished around 3,000 BC and is the oldest society that has left us clear evidence of angels in the form of stone carvings showing winged human motifs. The Sumerian religion was complex, embracing a wide variety of spirits and gods. Sumerians believed in messengers of the gods, angelic forces who ran errands between gods and humans.

Ancient Greek philosophy held that a god sent an *angelos*, or messenger, to watch over every individual. This messenger could be a human being or a spirit. *Malakh*, the Hebrew word for angel, also means messenger. This coincides with the Persian word for angel, *angaros*, meaning a courier.

Today, angels are still traditionally believed to be supernatural beings who act as messengers or mediators between the human world and God. Angels also have powers to perform works for God that are beyond the ability of humans.

Angels seem to be everywhere in popular culture. We see them viewed as guardians in television shows, movies, and books, and pinned to lapels. They are depicted as beautiful women with feathered wings or men of strength dressed in flowing white robes, and even as chubby babies with little wings.

Although angels take on different visual representations, missions, and powers, the one constant is that angels communicate with, minister to, and protect mankind.

Table of Contents

The angels are as perfect in form as they are in spirit. I die for speaking the language of the angels.

- Jeanne D'Ark

Joy

Betty Caithness

Fear not: for, behold, I bring
you good tidings of great joy,
which shall be to all people ...
And this shall be a sign unto
you; Ye shall find the babe
wrapped in swaddling clothes,
lying in a manger.

- Luke 2: 10,12

The Angel Carol

Rosemary West

The fruit of the Spirit is love,
joy, peace, patience, kindness,
goodness, faithfulness,
gentleness, and self-control.

- Galatians 5:22

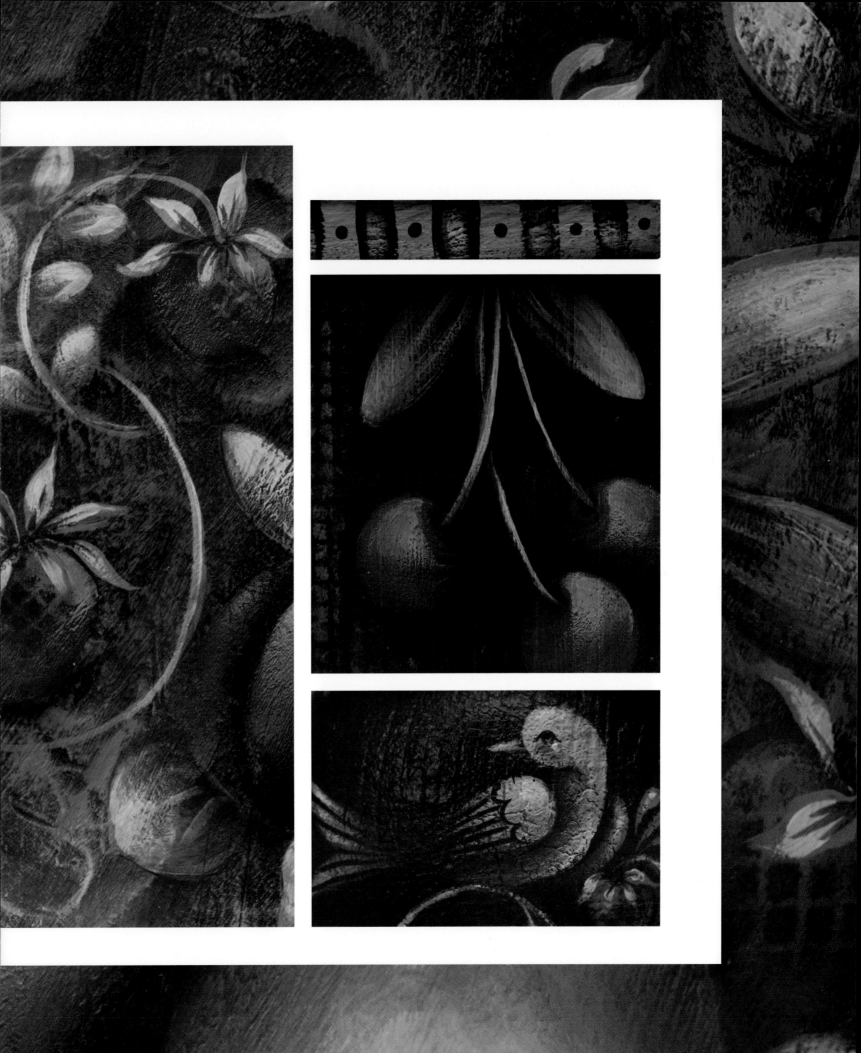

Coral

Sue Pruett

Country Angel

Barbara Nielsen

Angel of God,
My guardian dear,
To whom God's love
commits me here,
Ever this day,
be at my side,
To light and guard,
To rule and guide.

Angel
of
Tranquility

Marlene Kreutz

We are each of us angels with only one wing, and we can only fly by embracing one another.

- Luciano de Crescenzo

Jacquetta

Sharon McNamara Black

Jacquella has a knack for matching human hearts and homes with strays and rescue animals.

Scattering the Seeds of Love

Deb Malewski

I do not want to die ... until I have faithfully made the most of my talent and cultivated the seed that was placed in me until the last small twig has grown.

- Kathe Kollwitz

29

Angel

of

Springtime

Karen Hubbard

Delft

Angel

Judy Diephouse

Ark Angel

Lynne Andrews

Earth Angel

Jo Sonja Jansen

Earth Angel
Fresh Air
Clean Water
Nourishing Food

Patience

Sonja Richardson

Remember to leave room in your heart and garden for angels.

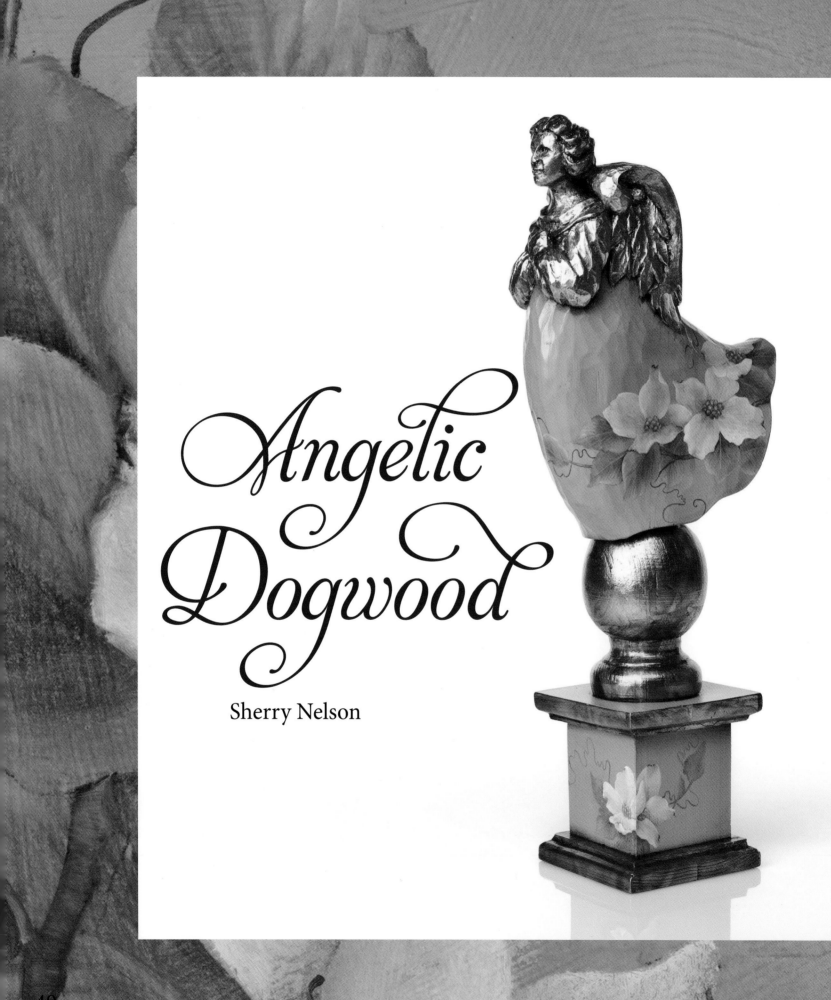

Angelic Dogwood

Sherry Nelson

To see a hillside white with dogwood bloom is to know a particular ecstasy of beauty, but to walk the gray winter woods and find the buds which will resurrect that beauty in another May is to partake of continuity.

- Hal Borland

Nature's Guardian

Kitty Gorrell

Within the vast expanse of our universe, there surely are many guardians to watch over the wonders of nature.

The Shepherd's Angel

Yvonne Kresal

O welcome, pure-eyed Faith,
white-handed Hope,
Thou hovering angel
girt with golden wings.

- John Milton

Lovely Lily

Cheri Rol

49

Folk Artists' Guardian Angel

Della Wetterman

When angels visit us, we do not hear the rustle of wings, nor feel the feathery touch of the breast of a dove; but we know their presence by the love they create in our hearts.

- Unknown

Quimper Angel

Peggy Harris

Heaven On Earth

Debbie Cotton

He who has not Christmas in his
heart will never find it under a tree.
- Roy L. Smith

Angelic Figurehead

Jo Avis Moore

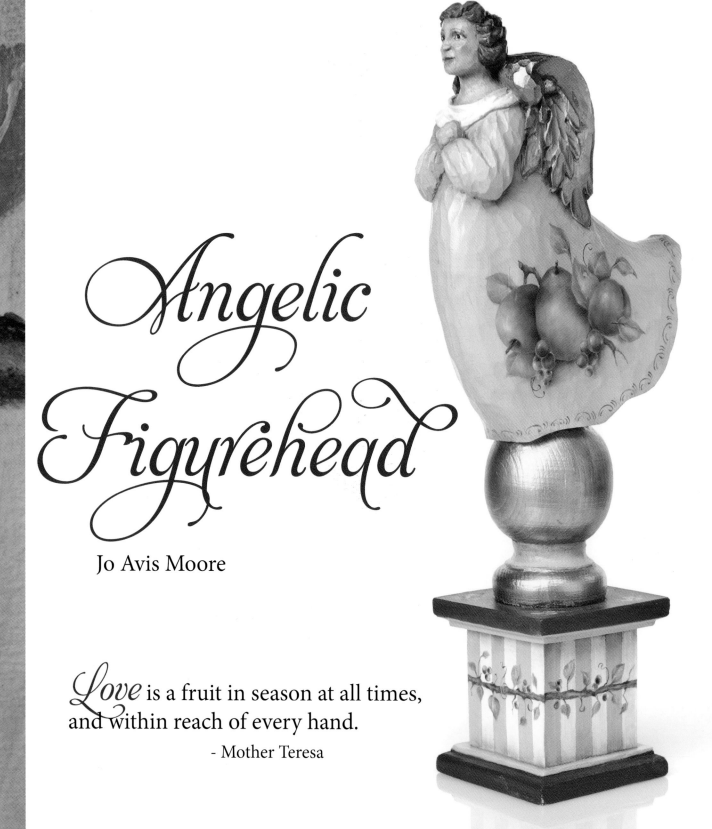

Love is a fruit in season at all times,
and within reach of every hand.

— Mother Teresa

Bella Sophia

Judy Westegaard

The name "Bella Sophia" means beautiful wisdom, a fitting name for this statuesque angel.

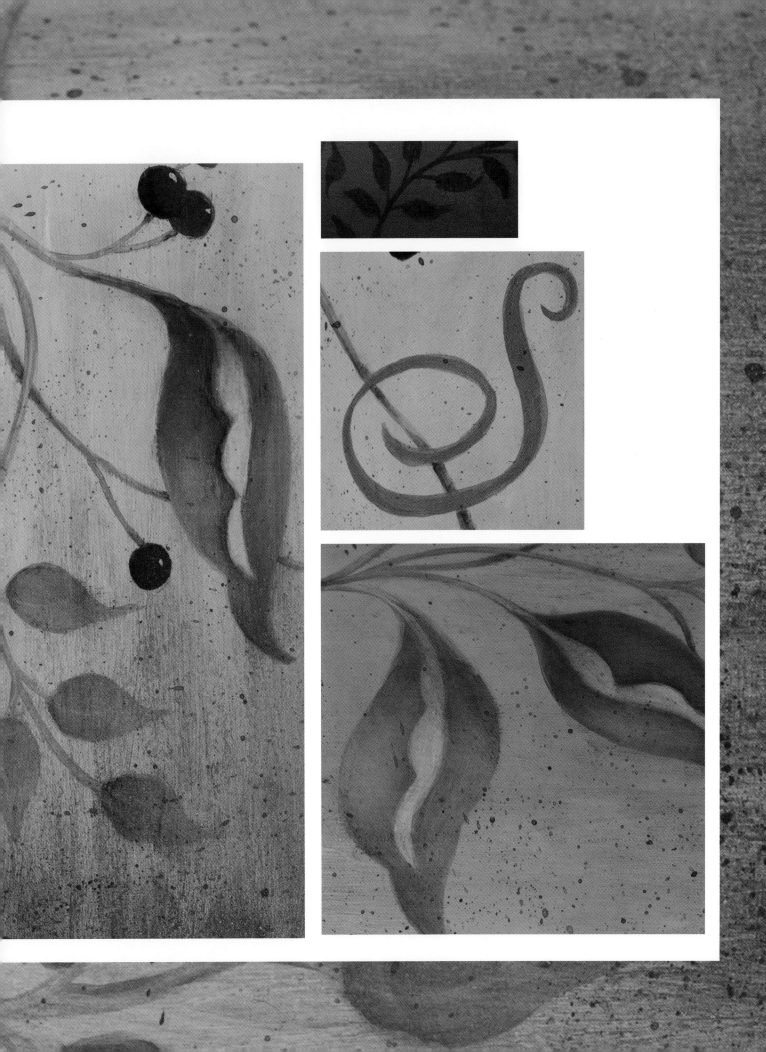

59

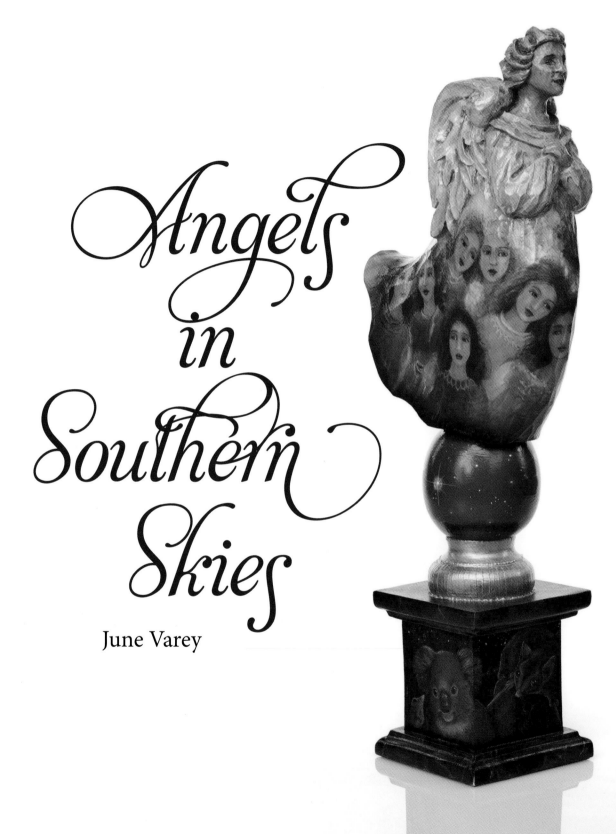

Angels in Southern Skies

June Varey

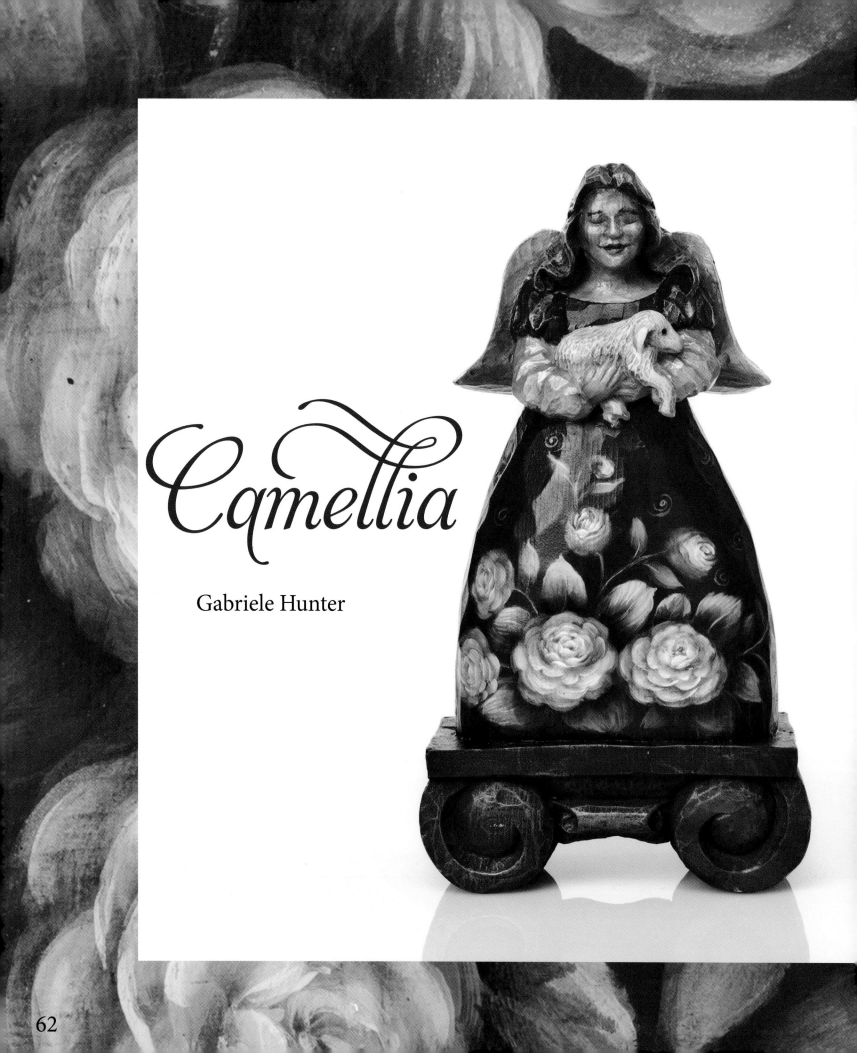

Camellia

Gabriele Hunter

Friendship Angel

Susan Abdella

Angel of Hope

Aileen Bratton

You can cut all the flowers but you cannot keep spring from coming.
- Pablo Neruda

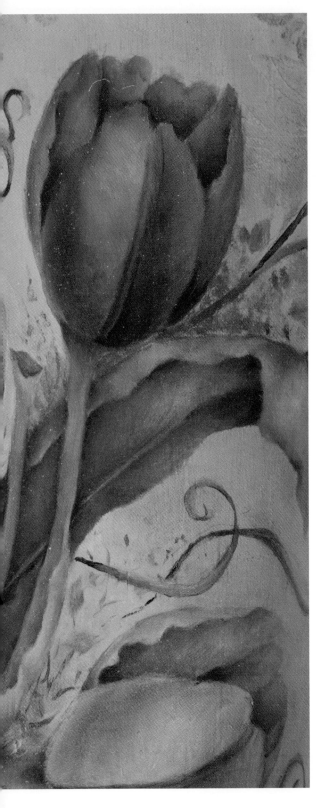

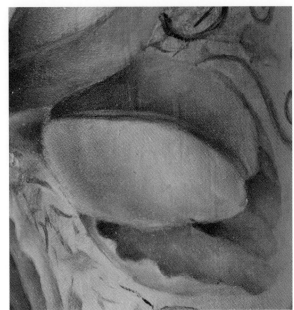

Terri Lea

Cindy Forsythe

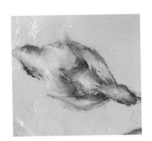

When hearts listen, angels sing.

- Anonymous

Treasured Memories Angel

Jamie Mills-Price

Vivian~
Paint with love!
Hugs
Jamie

These things I
warmly wish for you ...
A bit o' sun,
A bit o' cheer,
And a guardian angel
always near.

— Irish Blessing

Lori Liz

Beth Wagner

Serenity

Jeanne Downing

tulips have a message of hope, salvation by grace, redemption, and fellowship.

Nettie

Ginger Edwards

$\mathcal{I}$ believe kindnesses from others are angel touches.

No clouds gathered in the skies and the polluted streams became clear, whilst celestial music rang through the air and the angels rejoiced with gladness.

- The Buddha

Earth's Angel

Willow Wolfe

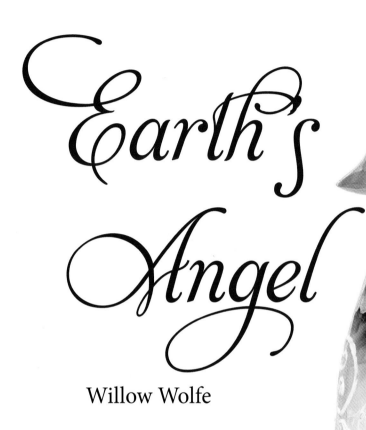

Earth's angel reminds us to slow our pace as we experience life and the gentility of the human spirit.

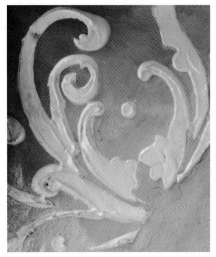

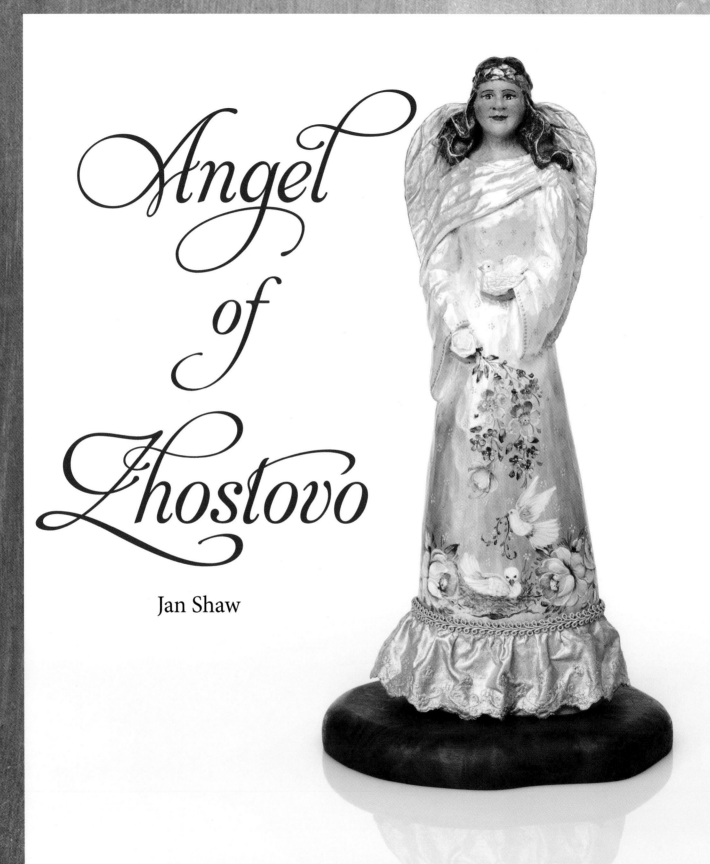

Angel
of
Zhostovo

Jan Shaw

Spring Floral Angel

Lynne Deptula

Herald of Spring

Gretchen Cagle

Holy Night Angel

Jim Shore

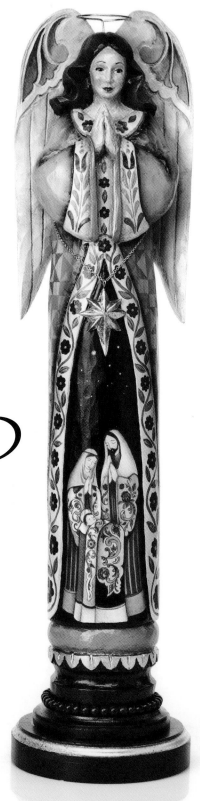

The angels announcing the wondrous event and then hovering joyously as our Lord is born is a beautiful vision. Suddenly a great company of the heavenly host appeared with the angel, praising God and saying, "Glory to God in the highest, and on earth peace to men on whom his favor rests."

-Luke 2:13-14

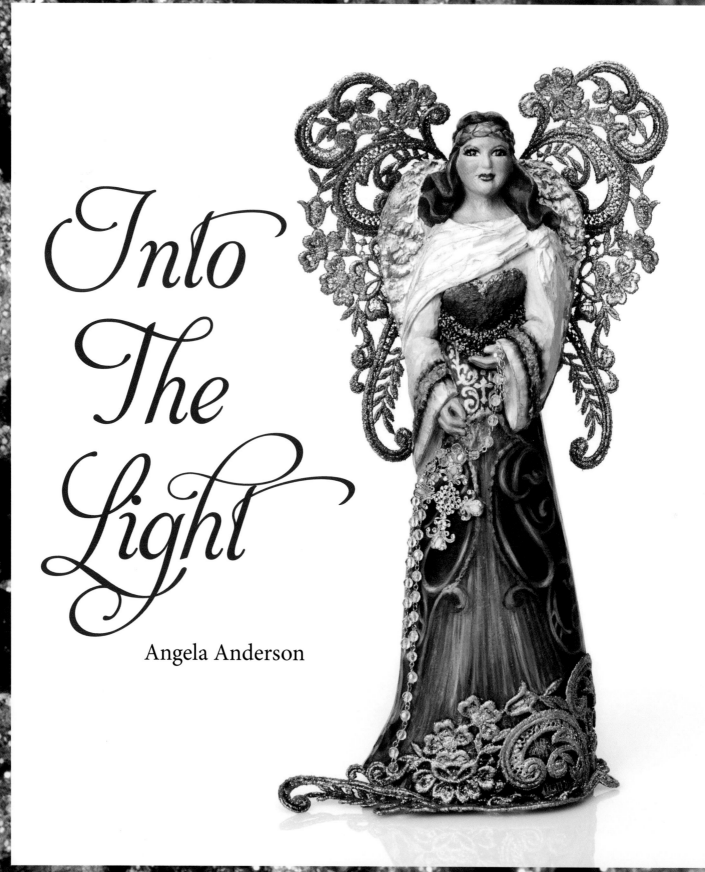

Into The Light

Angela Anderson

We shall find peace.
We shall hear angels,
we shall see the sky
sparkling with diamonds.

- Anton Chekhov

The Joy of Angels and Lambs

Helan Barrick

For he hears the lamb's
innocent call,
And he hears the ewe's
tender reply;
He is watchful while they are
in peace,
For they know when their
Shepherd is nigh.

- William Blake

Earth & Angel

Tom Jones

The beauty of nature is found in its imperfection rather than what is perfect. It is where I find peace; it is where I find angels.

Spring Lamb

Chris Thornton-Deason

Angel

Petals

Doxie Keller

There are always flowers for those who want to see them.

- Henri Matisse

Heaven Sent

Mary Jo Leisure

Heaven Sent displays a rich depth of color and beautiful delicate roses, which are my love.

Grace

Nancy Bateman

Grace was in all her steps,
Heaven in her eye,
In every gesture dignity and love.
    - John Milton

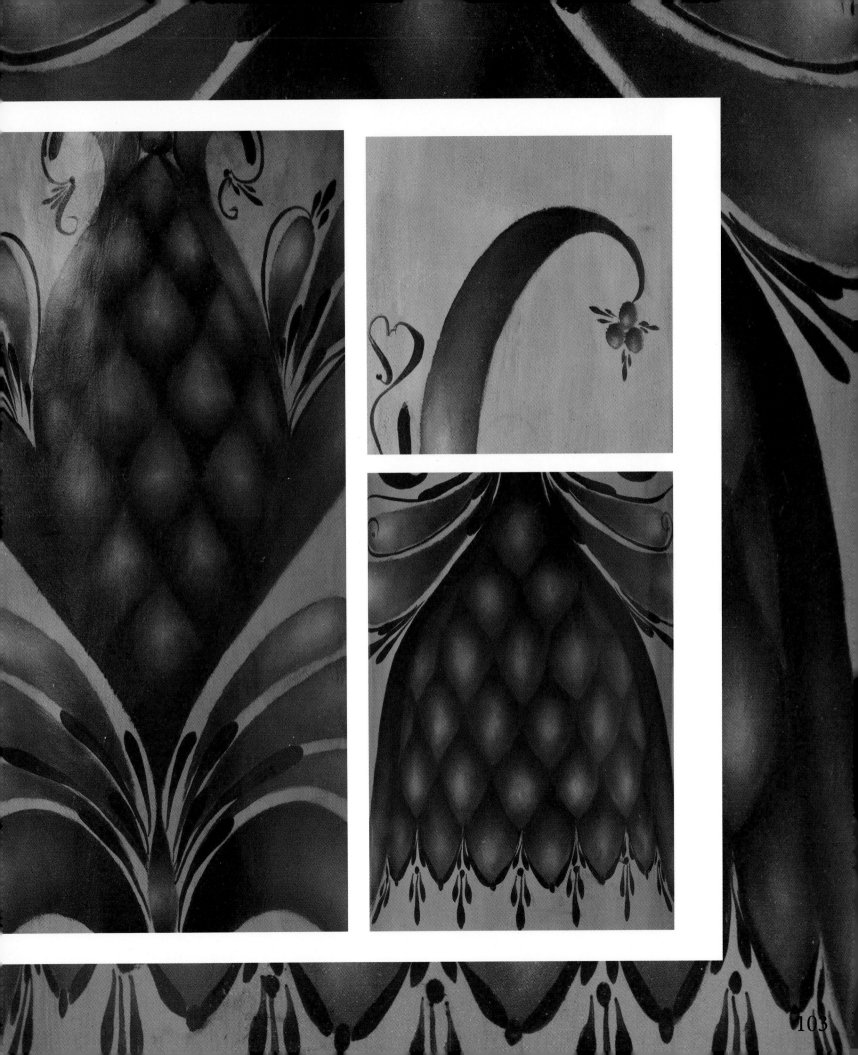

Angel
of the
Flowers

Marty Caldwell

I perhaps owe having become a painter to flowers.
  - Claude Monet

Wildlife

Angel

Mabel Blanco

It is not known precisely where angels dwell - whether in the air, the void, or the planets. It has not been God's pleasure that we should be informed of their abode.

- Voltaire

Angel
of
Spring

Trudy Beard

Spring signifies the cycle of life —
everything begins anew.

Angelic Roses Duet

Margot Clark

The world is a rose: smell it
and pass it on to your friends.
- Persian Proverb

A Mothering Angel

Kim Christmas

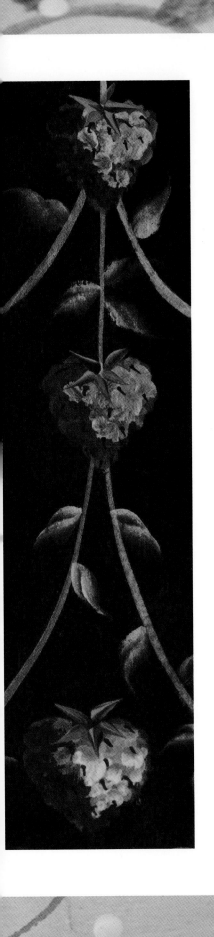

A Mothering Angel nurtures her children to grow and flourish under her watchful eye, just as a gardener keeps a watchful eye as he tends his garden.

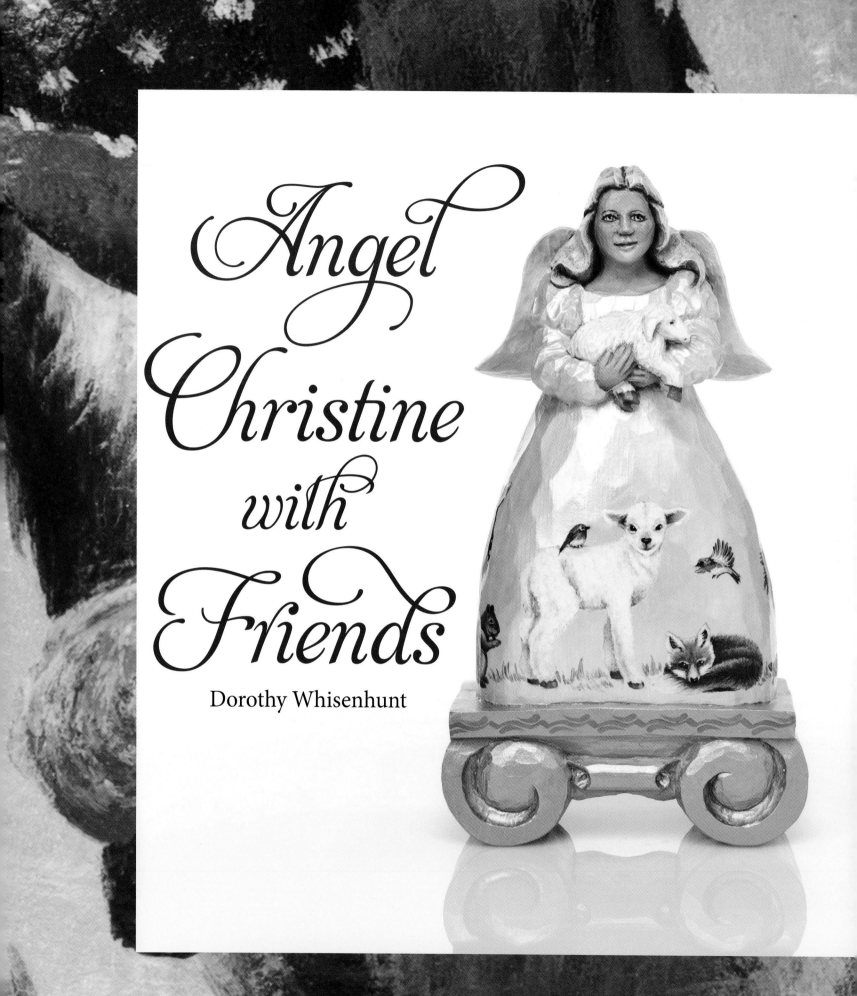

Angel Christine with Friends

Dorothy Whisenhunt

The Balance of Opposites

Kathie George

The masks represent the different faces an angel may have when she comes to us.

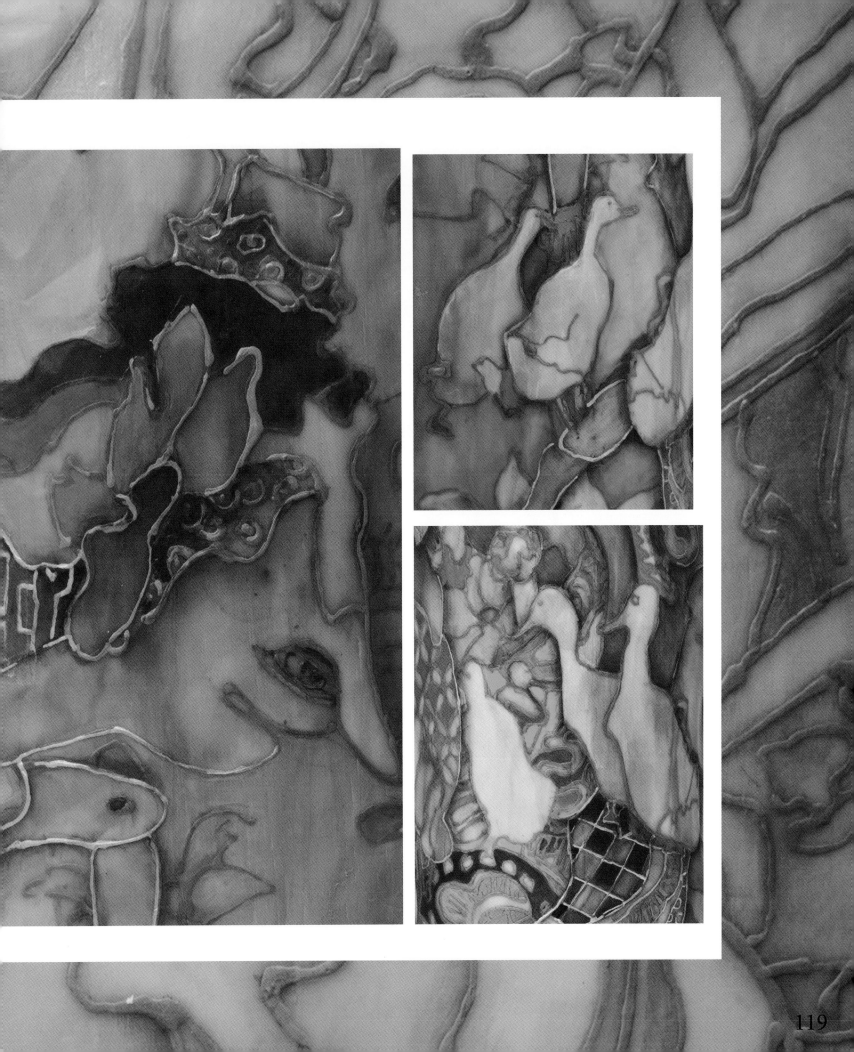

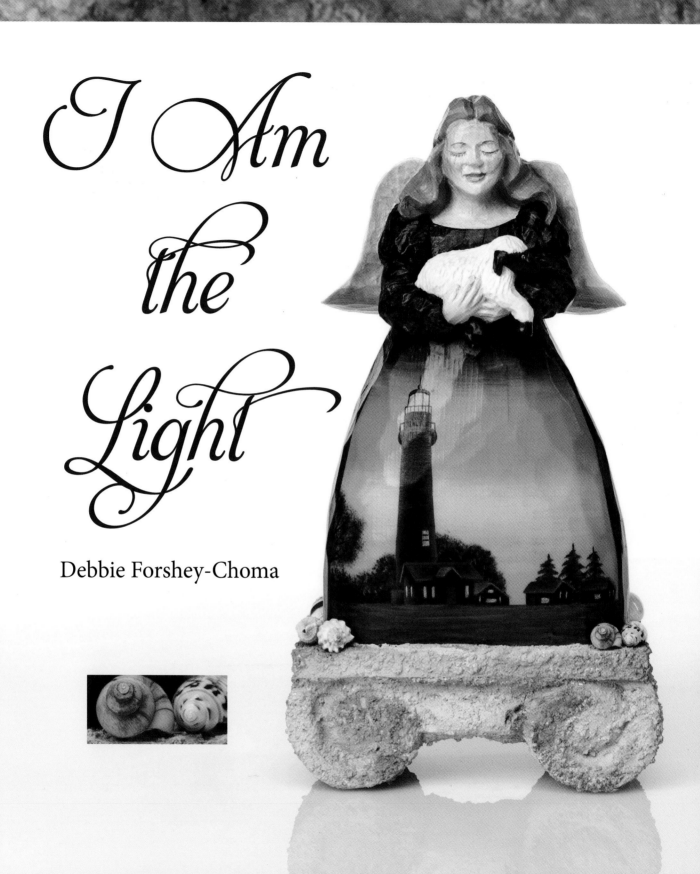

I Am the Light

Debbie Forshey-Choma

Walk while ye have the light,
lest darkness come upon you.
- John 12:35

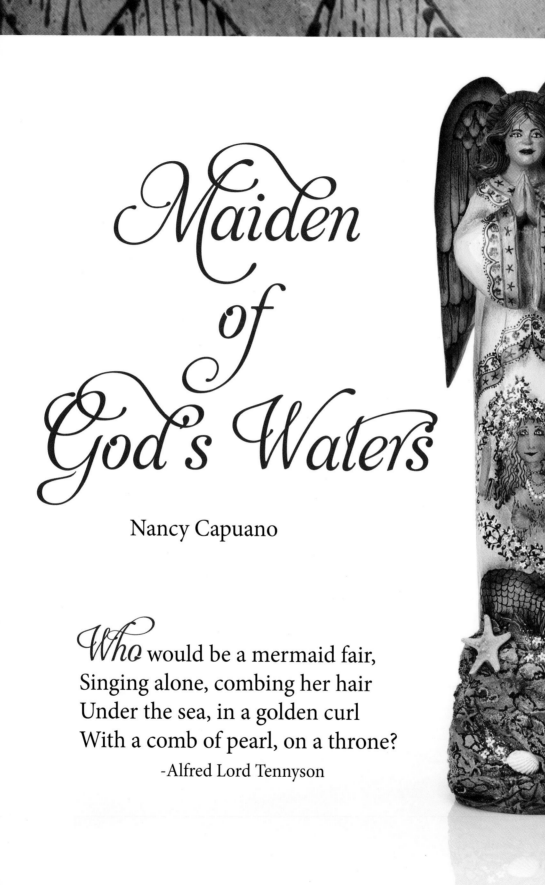

Maiden
of
God's Waters

Nancy Capuano

Who would be a mermaid fair,
Singing alone, combing her hair
Under the sea, in a golden curl
With a comb of pearl, on a throne?
-Alfred Lord Tennyson

Angel
of the
Harvest

Gloria Koskey

Cultivate the heart to raise a harvest of Truth, Righteousness, Peace and Love. This crop has to be raised in your heart and should be shared with others.

- Sri Sathya Sai Baba

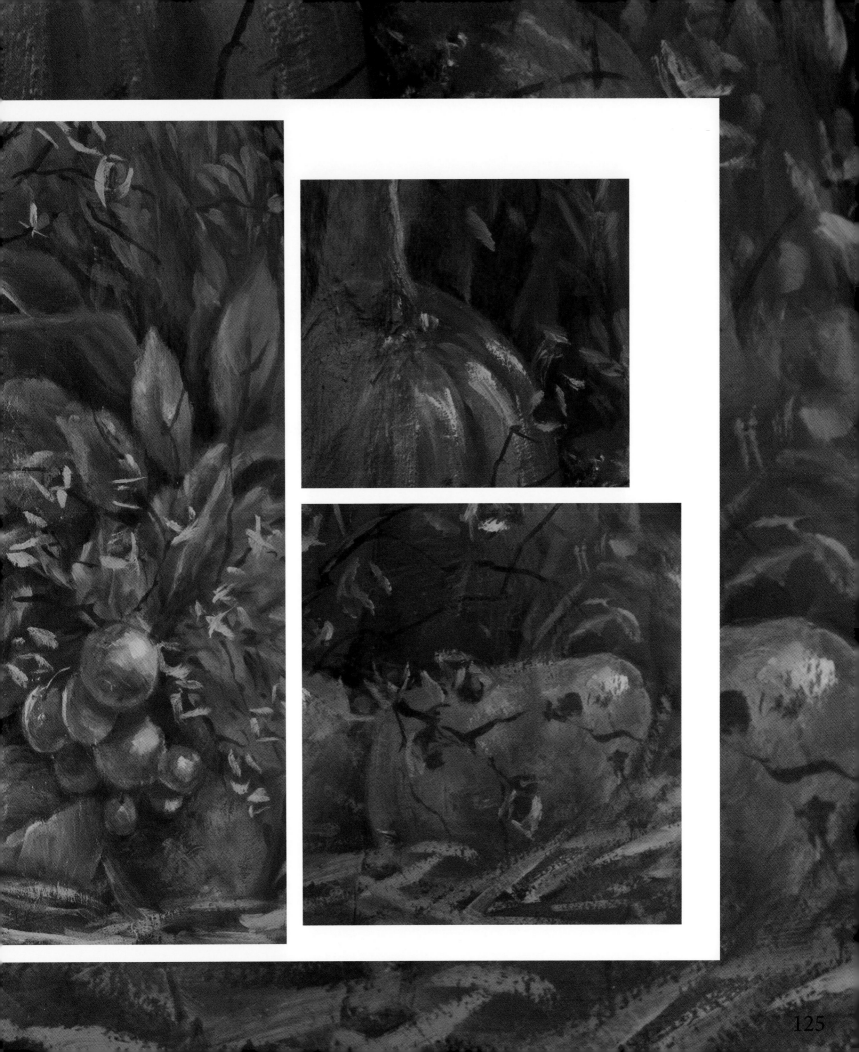

Angel
of the
Oklahoma
Plains

Judy Kimball

The beading represents Native American designs of the western plains of Oklahoma.

Flander's Angel

Tracy Moreau

In Flanders Fields the poppies blow
Between the crosses row on row,
That mark our place; and in the sky
The larks, still bravely singing, fly
Scarce heard amid the guns below.

        - John McCrae

Key Sake Angel

Janice Miller

Jenny

Toni McGuire

All of the people who knew her called her "Jenny." Only I was blessed with the distinct honor and privilege of calling her "Mother."

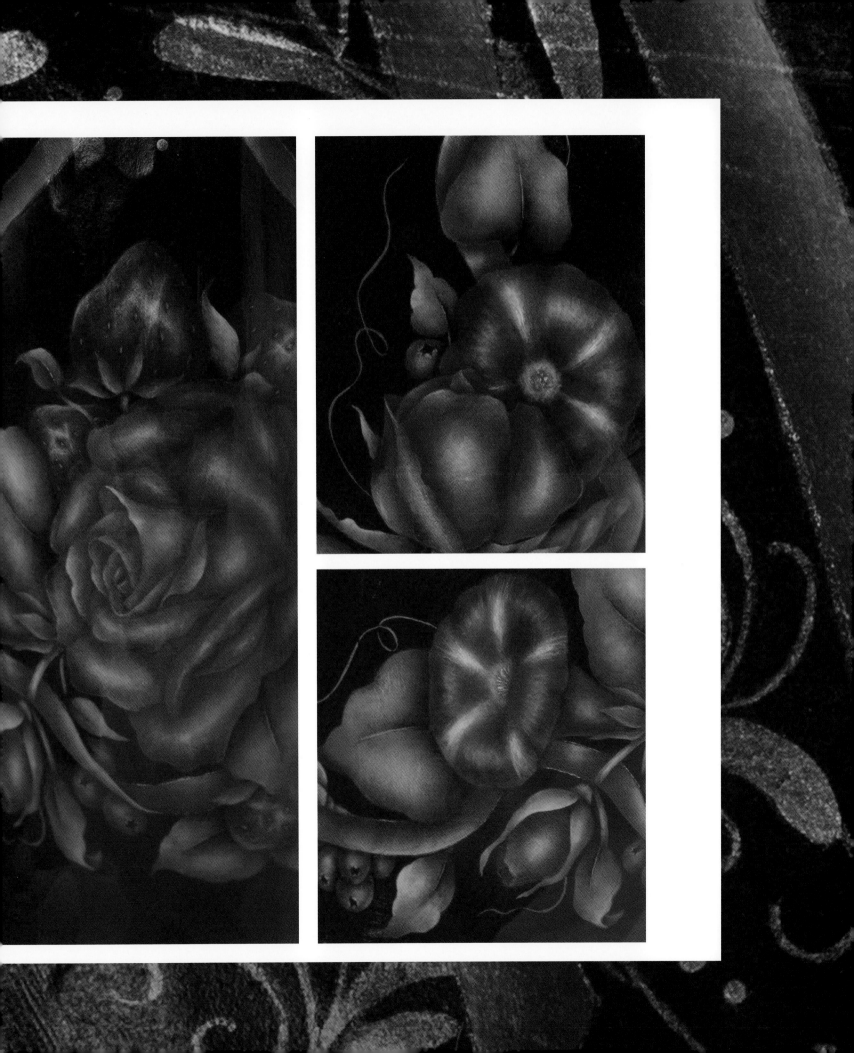

Simply Folk Art

Carol Payne

Regardless of the medium ...
In the best examples of folk art there
is a combination of naturalness and
simplicity, resulting in a directness
that has come to be much admired ...
- Robert Bishop

Earthly Protector

Jill Macfarlane

We do not inherit the earth from our ancestors,

We do not inherit
the Earth from our
Ancestors, we borrow
it from our Children.

- Native American Proverb

Shirley Anne

Maureen Calvert McNaughton

If we could see the miracle of a single flower clearly, our whole life would change.

- The Buddha

Garden Angel

Diane Bunker

Gifts from the
garden enrich
the soul ...

142

An angel can illume the thought and mind of man by strengthening the power of vision, and by bringing within his reach some truth which the angel himself contemplates.

- St. Thomas Aquinas

Lavender Angel

Louise Jackson

Angel

of the Universe

Kumiko Watabe

Caliel

Phyllis Gibbs

Do not whisper your name, we know it well. We have loved you forever, time will tell ...
We are your Guardian Angels.

- Anonymous

Peace Angel

Golda Rader

I am leaving you with a gift:
peace of mind and of heart.

Elegant Rose Angel

Ros Stallcup

Earth Angel

Joyce Beebe

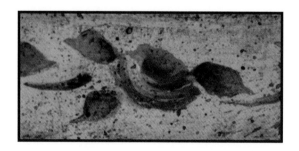

Angel
of
Creativity

Kim Hogue

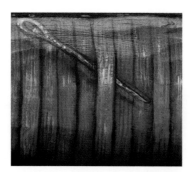

My Tennessee Angel

Betsy Thomas

Star of Wonder

Sharon Buononato

Star of wonder, star of night
Star with royal beauty bright
Westward leading, still proceeding
Guide us to thy Perfect Light

-Rev. John Henry Hopkins

Ellie

Lydia Steeves

Happiness is like a cat. If you try to coax it or call it, it will avoid you. It will never come. But if you pay no attention to it and go about your business, you'll find it rubbing up against your legs and jumping into your lap.

-William Bennett

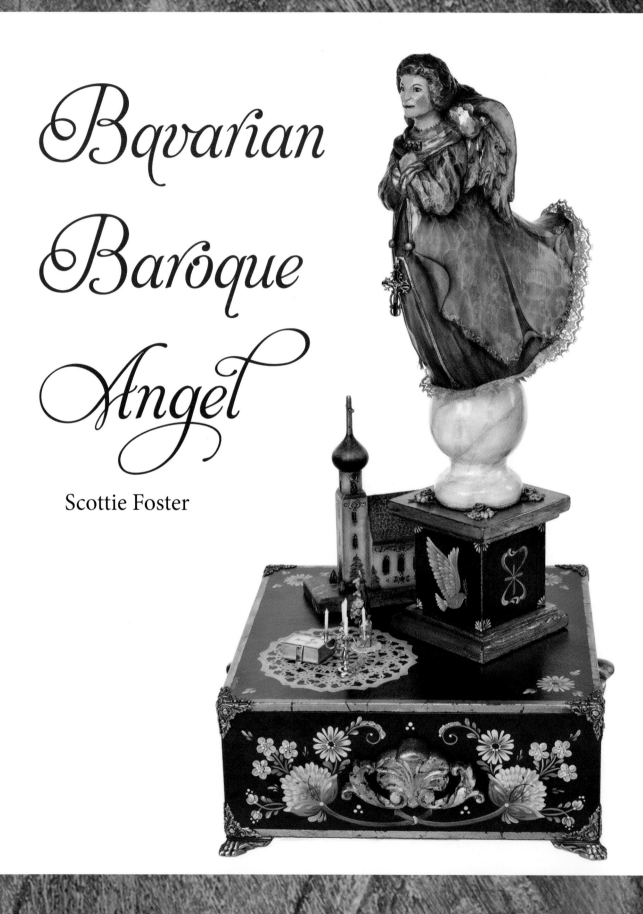

Bavarian Baroque Angel

Scottie Foster

Make yourself familiar with the angels, and behold them frequently in spirit; for without being seen, they are present with you.

- St. Francis de Sales

Weihnachtsengel

Heidi England

When I was a young girl, my German relatives sent a beautiful carved crèche to our home in Texas. Painting this angel brought back joyous memories of past Christmas celebrations and family traditions, many of which we still honor today.

Angel of the Garden

Mary Mader

The kiss of the sun for pardon,
The song of the birds for mirth,
One is nearer to God's heart in a garden
Than anywhere else on earth.

- Dorothy Frances Gurney

Angel Song

Cynthia Erekson

I rise up each day
with a song to the sea
and hope she will send you
back home to me.

172

I believe in angels —
They're always hovering near,
Whispering encouragement
whenever clouds appear,
Protecting us from danger
and showing us the way,
Performing little miracles
within our lives each day.

- Anonymous

The Farmer's Angel

Di Singleton

Be they kings, or poets, or farmers, They're a people of great worth. They keep company with the angels, And bring a bit of heaven here to earth.

- Irish Saying

Peace Angel

Shara Reiner

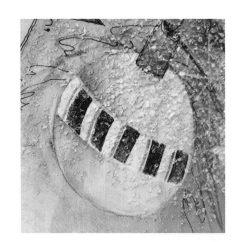

Tineke

Masayo Kunioka

There is nothing more difficult for a truly creative painter than to paint a rose, because before he can do so he has first to forget all the roses that were ever painted.

- Henri Matisse

Rose
of
Juno

Sharon Hamilton

Holly

Cindy Gensamer

Love came down at Christmas;
love all lovely, love divine; love was
born at Christmas, star and angels
gave the sign.

   - Christina G. Rossetti

Seven Sisters Angel

Carol-Lee Cisco

Blankets wrap you in
warmth, quilts wrap you in love.
- Unknown

Adrienne's Angel

Sandy Scales

Angels have to be quiet when they speak to you. They secretly whisper to you without anyone knowing.

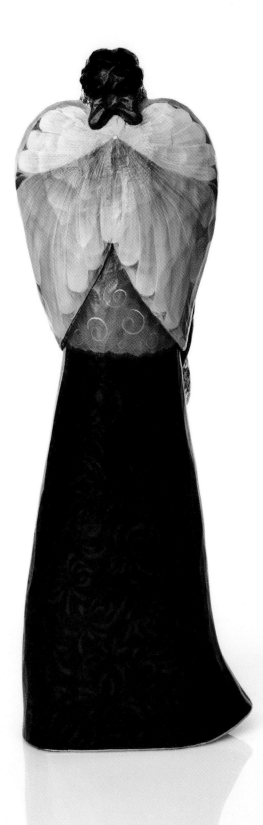

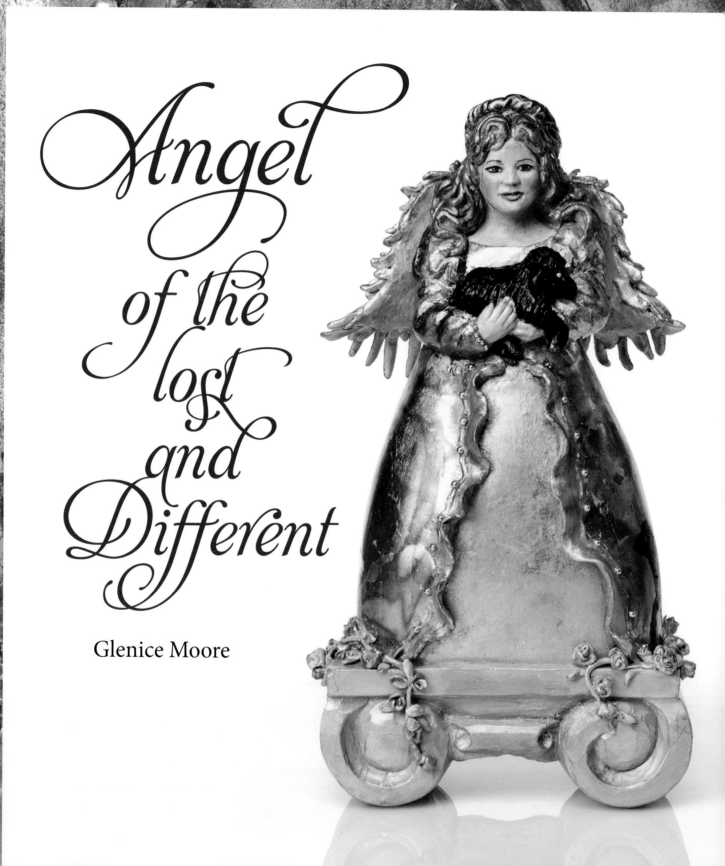

Angel
of the lost and Different

Glenice Moore

Where lambs have nibbled,
silent moves
The feet of angels bright;
Unseen they pour blessing,
And joy without ceasing,
On each bud and blossom,
And each sleeping bosom.

- William Blake

A Visiting Angel

Shirley Wilson

Peace I leave with you
My peace I give unto you.
- John 14:27

Seeds of Goodness

Kathi Hanson

Our acts of kindness plant seeds
of hope for those in despair.

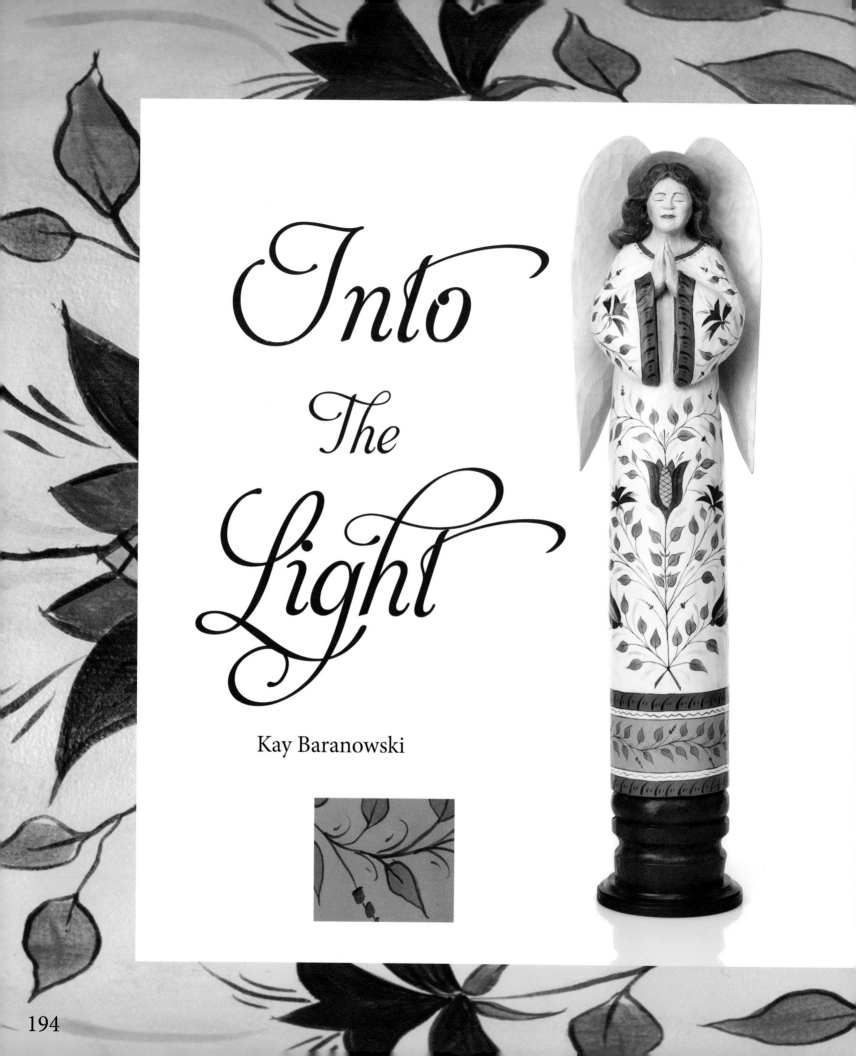

Into The Light

Kay Baranowski

When the light has sharply faded and you have lost your way, let another's love guide you. It can turn blackest night into day.

- Unknown

195

Thorns and Stings Strengthen Our Wings

Michele Walton

Autumn Angel

Tina Sue Norris

If you walk through the woods in fall, you cannot help but hear the autumn angels whispering.

Bounty

Andy Jones

Some partake of the bounty of the Lord's favor, which never runs out, while others receive only a handful. Some sit upon thrones as kings, and enjoy constant pleasures, while others must beg for charity.

- Sri Guru Granth Sahib

Baroque Holiday Angel

Linda Wise

Flor de Noche Buena - Flower of the Holy Night, the poinsettia, was thought by many in the eighteenth century to be symbolic of the Star of Bethlehem.

The Gift

Susan K. Stamilio

If instead of a gem, or even a flower, we should cast the gift of a loving thought into the heart of a friend, that would be giving as the angels give.

- George MacDonald

Who can know what tales are told in the whispers of an angel, Who can see what mighty deeds he does in the name of the Lord, What eye can see or mind can conceive of how he sees this world, Dark and light is angel sight. The battle brave, and souls are saved. Demons flee when we're set free, and angels there attend.

- Dennis Carlson Ragsdale

Gabriel Visits Norway

Gayle Oram

Music is well said to be
the speech of angels.
  - Thomas Carlyle

Susan's Garden Angel

Arlene Newman

You're only here for a short visit. Don't hurry, don't worry. And be sure to smell the flowers along the way.

— Walter Hagen

Consider The Lilies

Peggy Stogdill

Consider the lilies how they grow: they toil not, they spin not ...

- Luke 12:27

Guardian of Gardens

Prudy Vannier

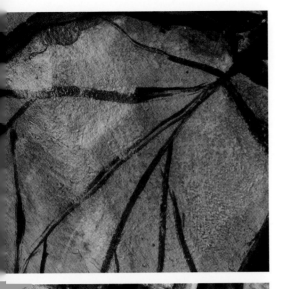

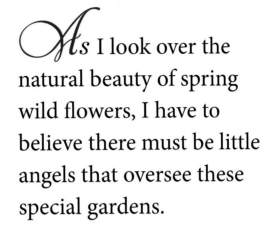

$\mathcal{A}$s I look over the natural beauty of spring wild flowers, I have to believe there must be little angels that oversee these special gardens.

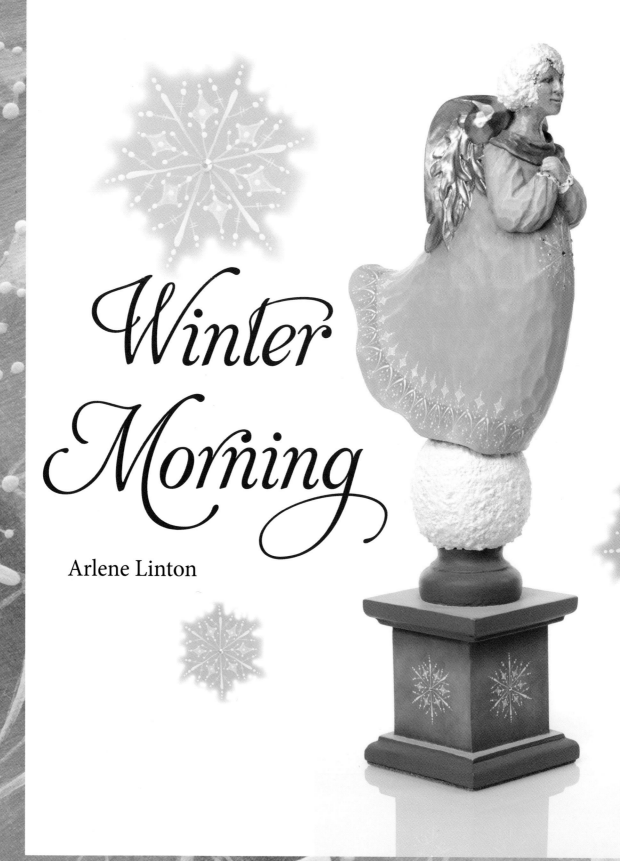

Winter Morning

Arlene Linton

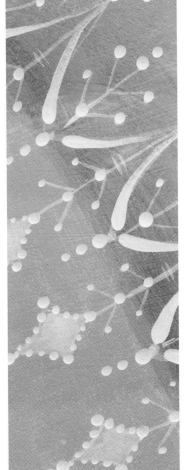

The air is perfectly still, the sky is brilliant blue, and the early morning sun makes the snow sparkle as if millions of diamonds have been tossed on the overnight snowfall.

217

Dorothee

Priscilla Hauser

Silently, one by one, in the infinite meadows of heaven, Blossomed the lovely stars, the forget-me-nots of the angels.

- Henry Wadsworth Longfellow

Nordic Angel

Lois Mueller

When angels touch us,
we are forever changed.

Wilderness Church Angel

Dorothy Dent

Peace
on
Earth

Heather Redick

May we live in peace without weeping. May our joy outline the lives we touch without ceasing. And may our love fill the world, angel wings tenderly beating.

- Irish Blessing

Peace Be With You

Maxine Thomas

Hail, thou that art highly favoured, the Lord is with thee: blessed art thou among women.
- Luke 1:28

Ordering Your Angel

These angels were handcarved by Kelley Stadelman, and then cast in high-quality resin. They are superb painting surfaces.

There are four unique styles of angels from which to choose. The tall angel is 26" tall; the angel on the finial is 18.25" tall; the shawl angel is 15" tall; and the angel with the lamb is 10.5" tall.

The angels can be ordered from All American Crafts, Inc., 7 Waterloo Rd., Stanhope, NJ 07874. Call 973-347-6900 ext. 115 to place your order.

Other Museum Publications

The National Museum of Decorative Painting is proud to present these publications based on past exhibitions and art in the Museum's collection.

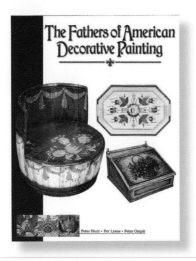

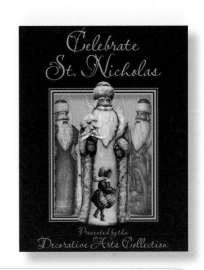

Visit www.dpmuseum.org to order these books and other delightful merchandise in the Museum's online shop.

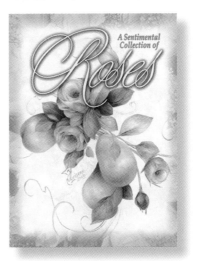

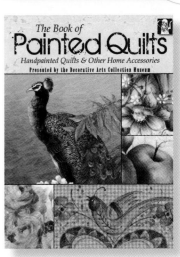

Contact the Museum at 404-351-1151 or visit us at 1406 Woodmont Lane NW, Atlanta, GA 30318.

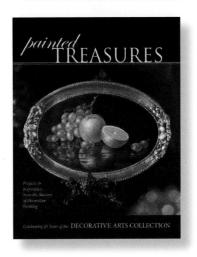

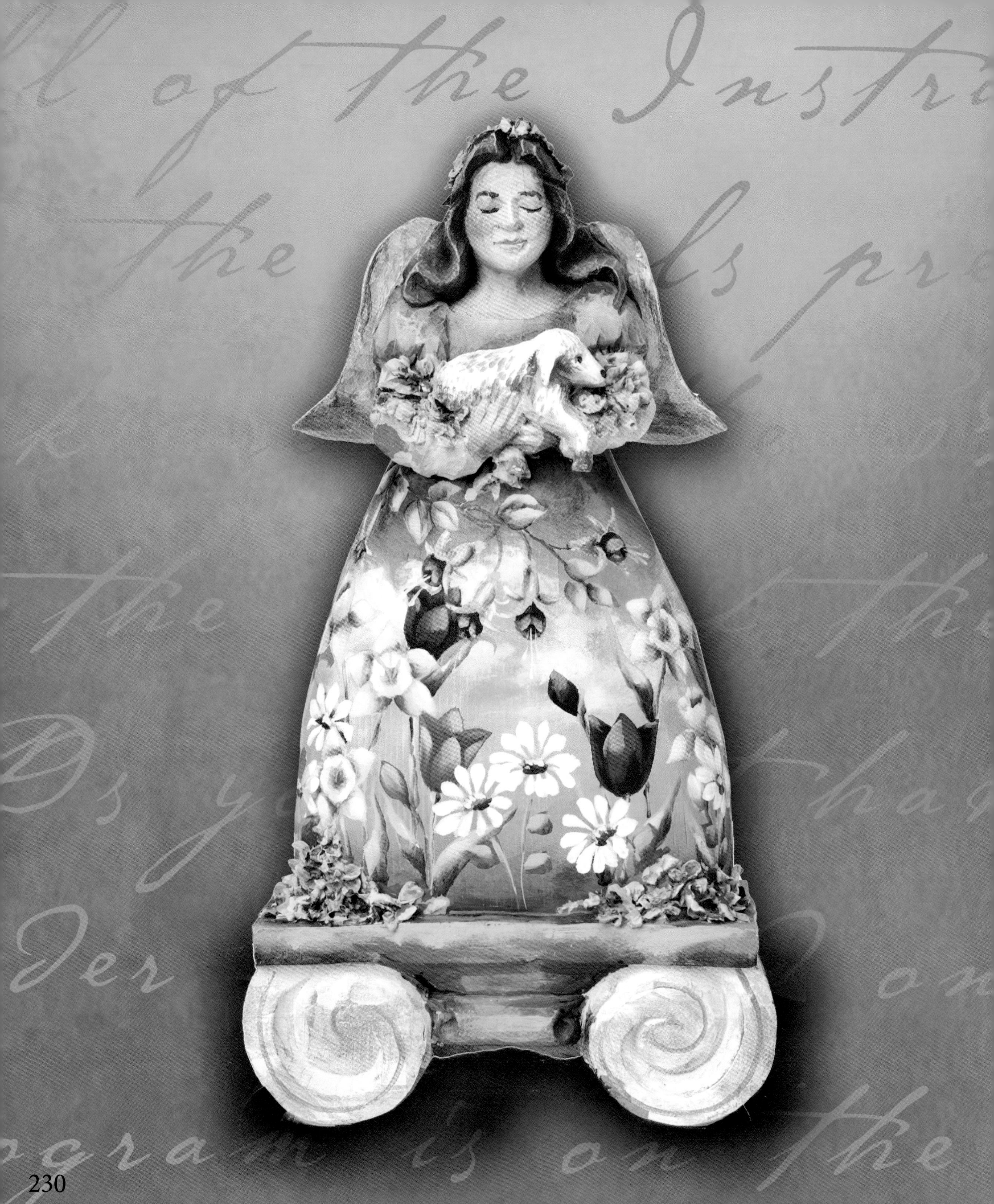

Instructional CD ROM

All of the instructions for painting the angels presented in this book are on the CD ROMS located in the back of the book.

To use these CDs, you must have Adobe® Acrobat® reader installed on your computer. The program is on the disc, if it is not already on your computer, and is compatible with both PC and MAC formats.

Simply place the CD ROM into you computer's CD drive and the file should automatically open. If it does not, just click the file name to open.

All of the instructions, full-size designs, and step-by-step worksheets are there for you. You may enlarge the images for easier viewing, and you may also print the designs for your personal use.

The CD ROMs are designed to work on a computer; they will not play on a DVD player.

Disc One

Betty Caithness

Rosemary West

Sue Pruett

Barbara Nielsen

Marlene Kruetz

Sharon McNamara Black

Deb Malewski

Karen Hubbard

Judy Diephouse

Lynne Andrews

Jo Sonja Jansen

Sonja Richardson

Sherry Nelson

Kitty Gorrell

Yvonne Kresal

Cheri Rol

Della Wetterman

Peggy Harris

Disc One

Debbie Cotton
Jo Avis Moore
Judy Westegaard
June Varey
Gabriele Hunter
Susan Abdella
Aileen Bratton
Cindy Forsythe
Jamie Mills-Price
Beth Wagner
Jeanne Downing
Ginger Edwards
Willow Wolfe
Jan Shaw
Lynne Deptula
Gretchen Cagle
Jim Shore
Angela Anderson

Helan Barrick
Tom Jones
Chris Thornton-Deason
Doxie Keller
Mary Jo Leisure
Nancy Bateman
Marty Caldwell
Mabel Blanco
Trudy Beard
Margot Clark
Kim Christmas
Dorothy Whisenhunt
Kathie George
Debbie Forshey-Choma

Disc Two

Nancy Capuano
Gloria Koskey
Judy Kimball
Tracy Moreau
Janice Miller
Toni McGuire
Carol Payne
Jill Macfarlane
Maureen McNaughton
Diane Bunker
Louise Jackson
Kumiko Watabe
Phyllis Gibbs
Golda Rader
Ros Stallcup
Joyce Beebe
Kim Hogue
Betsy Thomas
Sharon Buononato

Lydia Steeves
Scottie Foster
Heidi England
Mary Mader
Cynthia Erekson
Di Singleton
Shara Reiner
Masayo Kunioka
Sharon Hamilton
Cindy Gensamer
Carol-Lee Cisco
Sandy Scales
Glenice Moore
Shirley Wilson
Kathi Hanson
Kay Baranowski
Michele Walton
Tina Sue Norris
Andy Jones

Disc Two

Linda Wise
Susan Stamilio
Gayle Oram
Arlene Newman
Peggy Stogdill
Prudy Vannier
Arlene Linton
Priscilla Hauser
Lois Mueller
Dorothy Dent
Heather Redick
Maxine Thomas

237

238

239

Golden moments in the stream of life rush past us and we see nothing but sand; the angels come to visit us, and we only know them when they are gone.

- George Eliot